CW00531532

EVERYTI
YOU NEED TO KNOW
ABOUT BEING A KEYBOARD PLAYER!

by Geoff Ellwood

For Keyboards, Guitar, Drums, Bass Guitar & Saxophone.

Written by Geoff during the late spring of 1997. All music examples specially composed for the project.

Edited by: Clive Gregory

Assistant editor: J. Gregory

Photographs by Steve Collins

Artwork and design by Clive Gregory

Text and music typeset by R & C Gregory Publishing Limited

Imaging by Pulse Graphics Ltd, Kent, England.

Special thanks to: Rubiah Gregory, Peter Wall, Michael Pearse, Graham Mitchell, Ben Cooper, Mike Riley and Dan at Pulse and all at Colourscope, without whom this series of books would never have been possible.

First Edition published 1997

Published by
R & C Gregory Publishing Limited

Suite 7, Unit 6, Beckenham Business Centre, Cricket Lane, Kent. BR3 1LB.

ISBN 1 901690 12 1

Printed by CS PRINT & DISPLAY Limited, Croydon, England.

This book is dedicated to my wife, Lesley and children, Adam and Kate.

To be the wife of a musician is not, perhaps, the most enjoyable of paths to travel down in the search for marital bliss; so I'm taking this opportunity to thank my wife, Lesley who's unselfish attitude and huge support, in all my musical pursuits, has allowed me to really let my creative spirit run free!

Thanks also to Clive and Rubiah Gregory for their sincere belief and amazing energy to make things really happen.

Geoff Ellwood began his musical career at 15, originally as a Bass Player! He was working professionally by the time he turned 18 and toured extensively around the UK and Europe.

During this hectic time he gradually began to turn towards Keyboards and using these new found skills was able to quickly demonstrate a talent for song writing. This culminated in him being signed, first by E.M.I then Warner Bros and Chappel Publishing.

As a working professional and veteran of the gigging lifestyle, Geoff can often by seen leading his jazz rock outfit or working freelance.

He is a highly experienced and sympathetic teacher. He has for many years taught both Keyboards and Bass. His style of teaching is reflected in this book, a staunch believer that musical education is character building and of great benefit to all, regardless of ambition.

CONTENTS

INTRODUCTION

Ah! the Keyboard, the synthesiser , the Piano -what are they all about? Where do I start? What do I play? How can I achieve my goals?

If these are some of the questions you might be asking yourself, then read on...

THE MIDAS TOUCH

The learning of a keyboard instrument isn't always a fun thing to do. However, if you do possess a keyboard instrument then you are really in possession of a musical gold mine. With dedication, you can achieve both metaphorical gold (being able to play music *you* want to play) and also real gold by turning your new-found art into a business!

But gold doesn't come cheap. To find that gold you must be prepared to roll your sleeves up and dig hard for it. However, once you've extracted the gold, it will keep you musically and (if you're lucky) financially rich for the rest of your life!

So where do we begin to achieve our Midas touch?

First of all don't be scared of the instrument in front of you - it's just nuts and bolts and levers. You're the music. You're the controller. You're the master of your own musical destiny.

Here's my analogy:

Imagine a person working in a factory on their first day: Their job is pressing levers at

certain times which initiate a certain function which, in turn produces a specific result. Now on the first day the person is slow and confused -

"Was it *that* lever, or was it the other one?"

A week later, however, and their thoughts might be these:

"This is too easy and boring - I need something more challenging."

And that's how it is with keyboard playing: Levers depressed at certain times, in a certain order to produce a certain result - easy!

Throughout the book you will find 'teasers'. These short extracts may be quite difficult and are best learnt when you have completed the book.

the big purchase

the search

What to look for when shopping for a keyboard.

Firstly, the demo. This gives a pretty good indication of sounds on board. Don't, however, let the skilful arrangements blind your judgement and send you on a mad scramble to find your cheque book. Knee-jerk reactions in the shop now can be regretted at a later stage. So check out all the other keyboards in the shop and take your time.

the sounds

Try to have in mind which are the main sounds you'll be using most frequently - i.e. the Piano, the Strings, the Bass, the Drums and the Brass etc. Focus in on these sounds and try and determine which will be the best for you.

touch sensitive

It's also important to have a touch sensitive facility with the instrument. This means that dynamics will be registered due to lightness or heaviness of touch. In other words, if you play the keyboard lightly, it will respond to your touch and sound softer. Likewise, if you exerted more pressure it would sound louder. This is a useful facility to have, especially at performance level.

weighted keys

A keyboard with weighted keys will definitely be more expensive than one without this facility. On the plus side, though, are the benefits to be gained from playing such an instrument. Firstly, the hands will develop in much the same way as a conventional pianists' hands would. Secondly, performances on these instruments are much more conducive for allowing expression to be used to its maximum.

midi and other connections

Another important feature is the MIDI connections found at the rear of the instrument. MIDI (Musical Instrument Digital Interface) is used to link up to other hardware such as computers, sound modules, sequencers, drum machines etc. This is a very useful feature for composing at home as well as live work. There are usually three MIDI connections "IN" "OUT" & "THRU" which employ the 5 pin DIN method of connection. When connecting up to other hardware like a computer etc. make sure you refer to your keyboard and computer manuals - never use ordinary DIN leads, only use proper MIDI leads - mistakes can be costly!

input and output

Another feature you should have on the keyboard is input and output connections; input for bringing sounds into your keyboard from other external sources via their output. And output for sending your sound (signal) via a jack to jack lead to an external amplifier or mixing desk etc.

pitch wheel

The pitch wheel is a useful device for expression. Just as a lead guitarist uses the technique of bending his strings to give a more powerful, individual expression to his solo work, so too can we as keyboard players, use the pitch wheel to help along our expressive ideas. (Check out works by Chick Corea)

adsr

Here's an abreviation you will come across. The letters stand for:

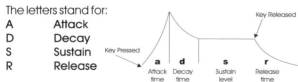

A	Attack	
D	Decay	
S	Sustain	Key Pressed
R	Release	

Key Released

a — Attack time
d — Decay time
s — Sustain level
r — Release time

These words refer to the 'envelope' of a sound. By appreciating that all sounds have 1) Attack (piano and percussion sounds have a fast attack, strings a slow attack), 2) Decay (the length of time the peak (attack) lasts until 3) Sustain (fairly obvious) and 4) Release; the length of time the note takes to 'die' once you release the key, you can effectively modify the sounds. Usually this is possible even on fairly humble synths. It is worth taking time to experiment with these basic parameters.

sustain

There should also be a facility for using a sustain pedal; you'll definitely need this for performance as well as recording smooth changes. You may not be supplied a pedal with the keyboard, so ask the salesperson to order you a pedal that will be the correct polarity for your particular instrument.

modulation wheel

The modulation wheel is used to put a vibrato or tremolo effect on your sound. This should be used sparingly and will take you a while to know when and where to use for its best advantage.

headphones

If you don't live on your own, the headphone socket will be good news for those living with you. Playing the theme from Eastenders a million times will try the patience of even your most ardent of friends. So do make use of this facility when others are around you

the musical alphabet

If you look closely at your keyboard you will see there are two groups or patterns that repeat up and down the instrument. These groups are a two black note group, followed by a three black note group. To locate the note C simply find the two note group and play its preceding white note. This note is C and this applies throughout the length of the keyboard. Now you know how to find C you can find any other note on the keyboard using the musical alphabet i.e. C - D - E - F - G - A - B /

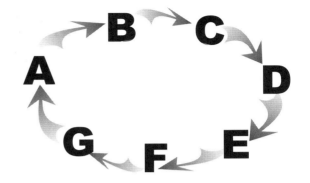

C - D - E - F - G - A - B / etc. make it your first duty to really know every note on your keyboard - you have the luxury of an easily recognisable layout - unlike guitarists and bassists who's job of learning their fretboard is quite a major task - suckers!

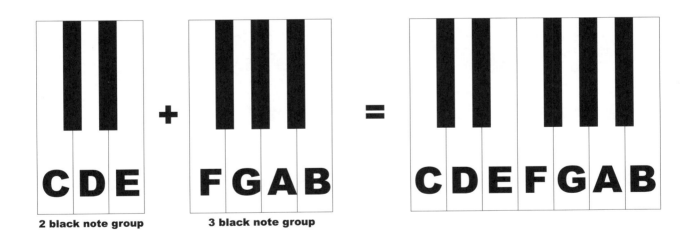

posture

Whether sitting or standing at your keyboard, you must be in a natural, comfortable position. It's no good leaning over your keyboard like some old jazzer who's almost playing notes with his nose. He's had three broken marriages, hooked on drugs and alcohol and probably hiding from the bailiffs - keep a check on your posture - don't slouch. Keep your back straight, arms and wrist relaxed. As a rough guide to a comfortable position, when your hands are placed on the keyboard your arms should be more or less parallel with the keyboard itself. When sitting don't use a bench use a high back chair, as sitting without support for any length of time can induce back strain.

expression

As you progress musically, you may feel that your body wants to join in on the act. Don't panic about this - you're now entering the world of expression! The differences between good performers and naff performers is not just keyboard technique: nine times out of ten the naff player will be working just one or two fingers on 'Top Of The Pops' - but he'll also be as stiff and inarticulate as a brick wall. Whereas the good performer will be using both hands, then fingers and, equally as important, his whole body to express himself and boost his performance. A keyboard player, like any other player who is rigid as a board, is about as visually exciting as paint drying. Don't force body movement - but don't restrict it if it comes naturally. You're the music - you're the controller - you're the master of your musical destiny.

understanding the examples

It's not always easy to understand from a book how to play examples and exercises. I have therefore decided to use a variety of devices to represent the examples and exercises you will need to learn. Read these two pages carefully, so that you can be sure of playing the right notes.

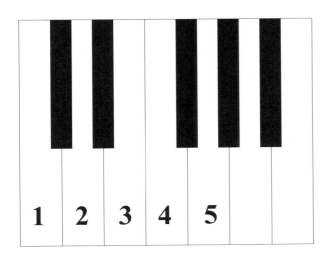

keyboard numbers

This style of notation is useful for short exercises where the order or sequence of notes is most important.

Remember, the numbers represent the order in which you play the keys.

keyboard graphic

The keyboard graphic is especially useful when explaining chords. The example opposite makes it easy to see which notes you press down (at the same time) to play the chord of C major.

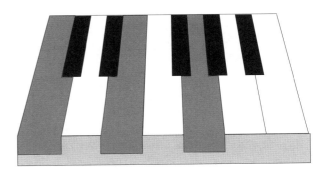

photographic

There is rarely a good substitute for seeing how your hands should be looking. So I will use a photograph to reinforce other forms of notation.

Photographs are really useful when trying to further illustrate technique.

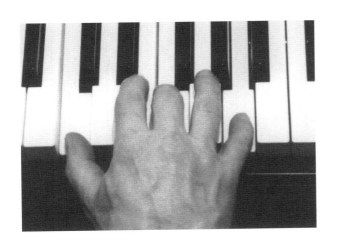

chromatic ladder

The chromatic ladder is the main means by which I'll explain chord construction.

Although the opposite example shows the chromatic ladder beginning on C, the ladder can be started on any note.

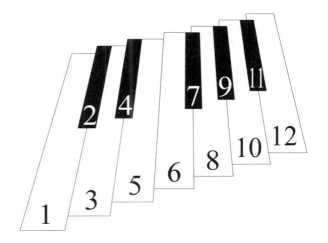

standard music notation

Eventually you will rely more and more on standard music notation. Although it looks difficult at first it is actually an excellent way to convey musical ideas.

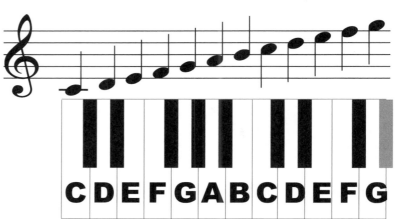

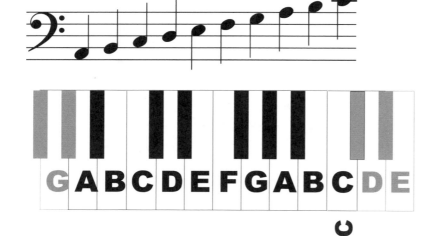

The examples on this page are only meant to show you how the notes on the music staff relate to the notes on your keyboard.

Don't worry, they'll be more on this subject later in the book.

GETTING TO KNOW YOUR HANDS

keeping musically fit

Like any other form of fitness training, exercises play an important role in achieving this aim.

Brain to finger response is made so much easier if the muscles and joints are pre-conditioned. To act upon the information transmitted from brain to finger-tips a sense of 'oneness' is vital and not a sense of strangeness that you may, or may not be experiencing at this moment.

transmission

Place your right thumb on middle C of your piano/keyboard (i.e. the C note that is in the middle of your keyboard). Now make sure your four remaining fingers hover over the four successive white notes (D-E-F-G).

All I want you to do now (and I'm not patronising you) is to simply press down with your thumb whilst keeping your other fingers lightly touching their respective notes. Now lift your thumb and press your index finger down on its note (D). Work your way along until you reach your little finger (G) and work your way back again to your thumb (C).

This must be executed in a slow, methodical manner to begin with; the object being to really feel where those lines of transmission are in your arm, wrist, hand, fingers and finger-tips. Don't be misled; many students can't get this down even though they've been fiddling about on a keyboard for months. By doing this exercise NOW, first right hand then left, then both hands at the same time, you'll be getting the best possible grounding you can have for good technique playing and brain to finger understanding.

(See the keyboard number example on the next page.)

transmission - keyboard number example

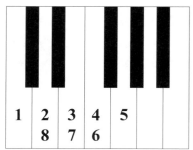

right hand

left hand

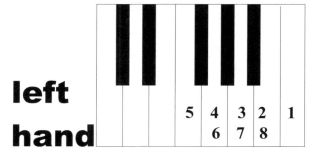

independence day (for your fingers)

Perhaps I'm being cruel here but this exercise sorts the men from the boys. Visually it looks patronisingly simple and you might choose to skip it; but first just give it a go, you'll wish your brain was a little more in touch with your fingers!

As in the transmission exercise, place your right thumb over middle C and rest your remaining fingers on their successive notes (D,E,F,G) this time two fingers work together whilst the other three rest. So press down C with the thumb (1st)

and the E with the middle finger (3rd) whilst keeping the other three fingers just lightly touching their respective notes (D,F,G) Now I want you to slowly release the C and E but start to press your index (2nd) and ring finger (4th) down. Now release 2 and 4 but this time press down middle finger (3rd) and little finger (5th) then release 3 and 5 and press 2 and 4. This finishes one cycle. Repeat the cycle 5 or 6 times then try the exercise on your left hand; here's the fingering: 5th and 3rd, 4th and 2nd, 3rd and 1st, 4th and 2nd, repeated 5 or 6 times.

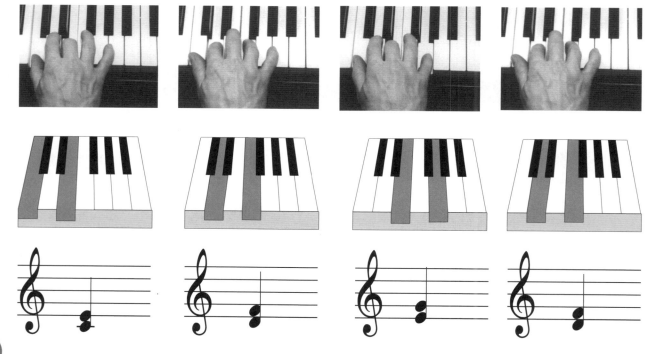

broken thirds

This exercise builds up dexterity to each individual finger.

Place your right hand as in the 'transmission' and 'independence day' exercises but this time press your thumb down on C then release and press middle finger on E. Release and press index finger on D release and press ring (4th) finger on F, release and press middle finger on E - release and press little finger on G release and press index finger on D. Finally, to complete the cycle, release and press ring finger on F then repeat this over a few times gradually increasing speed. Then try the same exercise but using your left hand. If you feel adventurous try both hands at the same time.

There are numerous other exercises you can do but repetition of these three on a daily basis will prepare you for the real world.

Any musician worth his salt will regard his/her fingers with much reverence. Really getting to *know* your hands and fingers - what they can and what they can't do - will help put your musical goals in a clearer perspective. Take the opportunity to look at other advanced musicians' hands. See how alive and expressive their hands are - even away from their instrument!

Constant practise and general playing can only achieve this fascinating characteristic. You can achieve this too!

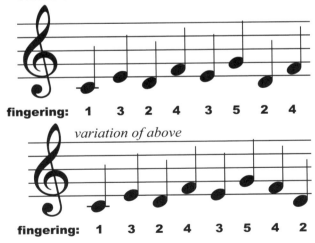

"teaser"

chords

No, they're not unfashionable trousers that a university lecturer might choose to wear. Chords are simply a family of notes.

"But they're confusing, how do I remember them all?"

Well, by the illustration below, you can see where C is, so lets call him Dad. The head of the family is named after him - the C family. But what if we want to know the name of his wife or his son? What then? Well, we simply climb the chromatic ladder. Dad is always at the bottom of the ladder, so he's number 1. To find his wife you simply move up the ladder until you land on note 5 (E) and to find her son you simply land on note number 8 (G). This way you can find any family on the keyboard - easy eh? Remember, all you need to know is the family name and then you can quickly work out who mum and her son are.

Now, these families are all happy families and give off happy vibes, but that's not a very scientific term so they labelled the family the MAJOR family. There is, however, another family that gives out a sadder vibe, which the gods of music have called the MINOR family. To construct this chord or family you only have to worry about finding mum - instead of 5 steps up the chromatic ladder she can now be found four steps above Dad (The Root). The son stays where he is at 8 above Dad. So the notes for C minor are C E♭ (E flat) and G. The only change you make from Major to Minor is lowering the middle note.

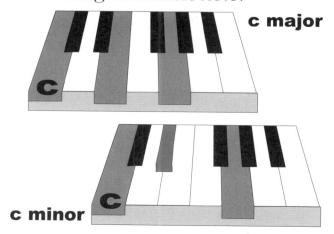

c major

c minor

expanding the chord family

We've established our basic major and minor families but there are further additions that can be added to these families. The most common being the 7th. Whether it be major or minor the 7th is the same note for both families. Let's continue the family theme and call our 7th the daughter - how can we find her? Well, Dad is 1, Mum is 5 (major) or 4 (minor) the son is 8 and the daughter is 11. This is a guaranteed simplistic way of locating notes and turning them into chords. If you are a raw beginner then have fun for a couple of weeks using busking books that have your favourite songs in. Keep trying to focus on the whereabouts of certain chords - enjoy your musical journey.

inversions

Hopefully we've got a good idea about the formation of chords both major and minor. But using this formation of root (R) third (3) fifth (5) is very cumbersome when it comes to changes i.e. going from say C major to F major. It can be done but it sounds jerky and amateurish. So how do we solve this problem?

The answer is inversions: to invert the notes that make up the chord. So let's take the problem of going from C major to F major. We'll start C major using the 1 3 5 method, root - C, third - E, fifth - G. Now, to change smoothly to F major we first of all see which note(s) we don't have to change because it (or they) might be in the next chord - i.e. the note C is in both C major and F major - so we can hold the thumb on C whilst moving the other two fingers and placing them smoothly on notes F and A. You can see how useful this device is. The study of inversions is the most beneficial thing you can do. Our job, as Keyboard players, is to be an unnoticed layer of sound without jerkiness or interruption.

The only way to achieve this is the study of inversions. The word study can be off-putting; perhaps another way of putting it is learn-as-you-go, this is the way I myself learnt about inversions. Simply by going through the busking books and learning the chords of a song using the inversion method i.e. no big jumps from chord to chord, I soon built up a recognition of all possible inversions; thus allowing me to be able to take my eyes off the keyboard and still know exactly where I am and what chord I'm playing. After a few weeks practising this method you'll start to really see the chords come to life before you. Persevere - you'll get there.

chordal cousins

There are another two families you will have to learn once you've understood major and minor, these are:

diminished
the 'eerie' family

This chord, when played, has a sort of expectancy of something sinister that's about to happen. The formula is easy to remember. If the chord is C diminished seventh, we would have to play the notes C - E♭ - G♭ and A. On the chromatic ladder C would be 1, E♭ would be 4, G♭ would be 7 and A would be 10, see fig. 1. The interval from one note to another is the same: a minor third. C diminished can also be played without the A (miss out 10 on the ladder).

This chord may not crop up all that often but it's worth getting to know the sound and quality that the chord produces.

augmented
the 'guiding you home' family

To augment a chord is to raise one of the notes. The note raised when we see the chord symbol C aug or C+ is always the 5th note of the scale or, using the family theme, it's always the 'son' that's promoted a semitone higher from G to G♯ or from 8 on the ladder to 9.

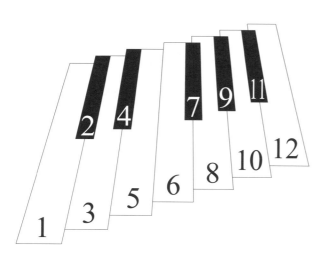

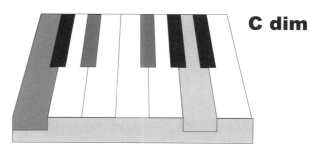

C dim

fig. 1

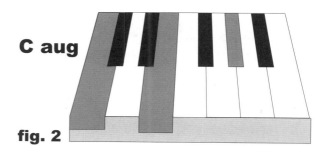

C aug

fig. 2

SETTLING DOWN
THE RHYTHM OF LIFE

back to school

There comes a time in music when we have to team up with mathematics and even a little science.

To kick off the maths lesson I simply want you to tap your foot once and on this beat count aloud in an even manner 1, 2, 3, 4 (slowly) here's what it looks like musically

<u>WHOLE NOTE = 4 Beats</u>

O   O

1 2 3 4   1 2 3 4

Once you've mastered that, try tapping your foot on beats one and three; here's how this looks when written down:

<u>THE HALF NOTE = 2 beats</u>.

1 2 3 4   1 2 3 4

Now try tapping your foot on each beat as you count 1, 2, 3, 4; here's how that looks:

<u>THE QUARTER NOTE.</u>

1   2   3   4

Next, try counting 1, &, 2, &, 3, &, 4, & here's how this looks written as music; these are called eighth notes or 'eights'.

<u>EIGHTH NOTES</u>

1 & 2 & 3 & 4 &

There are other divisions - but I'm sure you're beginning to get the picture.

The arithmetic divisions of rhythm - at a glance!

$1^e \&^a 2^e \&^a 3^e \&^a 4^e \&^a 1$

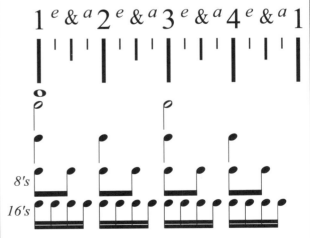

8's
16's

The groups of 4 notes with 2 beams are sixteenth notes - they are counted 1 e & a, 2 e & a, 3 e & a, 4 e, & a.

importance of silence - rests

It is equally important to know about rests or silences. Although notes are quite easy to hear if you've got it right or not, with rests there is nothing to hear, is there?

Yes there is!

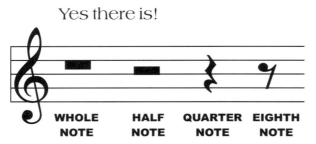

WHOLE NOTE   HALF NOTE   QUARTER NOTE   EIGHTH NOTE

Silence is very much hand in glove with sound and should be treated equally. You must familiarise yourself with the symbols of rests and their meaning.

symbols of silence - the rest symbols!

When practising these exercises, count evenly and ensure that your fingers are off the keys when the count is under a rest symbol. At the point of the rest symbols there must be SILENCE!

the tie

This is a curved line that connects two successive notes of the same pitch and unites them into a single sound equal to their combined durations. It has three uses.

1. To connect two notes separated by a bar line. (fig. 1)
2. To produce values that cannot be indicated by a single note on its own. (fig. 2)
3. To illustrate beat groupings, making music easier to read. (fig. 3)

In this first figure, the tie is used to enable a note to sustain 'through' a bar line; i.e. the sound sustains from beat 3 of the first bar, through to beat 3 of the second bar.

Figure 2 shows how a tie can create a length of sound that cannot be expressed as a single symbol. In this case the sound is equal in length to 5 eighth notes.

In figure 3. the tie is used to allow the eye to easily locate each beat (grouped here in pairs of eighth notes). This makes reading at sight much easier.

the dotted note

When a dot is placed after a note head, the length of that note is increased - BY HALF! e.g. a dotted half note is equal in length to a half note and a quarter note.

The following examples should make the function of the dot clear. Follow the counting carefully to make sure you understand.

In the example below, notice that whereas the normal quarter note lasts for 2 eighth note counts, the dotted quarter note lasts for 3 eighth note counts (one + half).

1&2&3&4&   1&2&3&4&

1&2 & 3&4 &   1&2 & 3&4 &   1 & 2 & 3 &4&

Careful with the above; dotted notes and tied notes!

time-keeping

Playing in time is a necessary criteria to being an able musician.

Never believe (like so many amateur musicians) that you have, or were born with, perfect time. Always use a metronome or drum machine when you practise your pieces.

If you are using a metronome with a bell, let the bell strike on the 1st beat. This will keep a check on your timing through the piece. If you are using a drum machine have the kick drum on the 1 beat the snare on beats 2 and 4 and have the closed hi-hat playing eighth notes throughout. I.e. 1 & 2 & 3 & 4 &.

Of course you'll have to vary these settings for other timings such as ¾ 5/4 7/4 9/8 etc. but for all your 4/4 pieces, and most of the exercises you'll play, this will be a good standard setting to use.

time signatures

Time signatures convey visually what we hear in the rhythmic grouping of music. Rhythmic grouping is heard as accented (slightly louder or stressed) notes.

Time signatures simply relate to you how many beats there are in a bar and what the value of those beats are. For instance, the most common time signature is 4/4. When we see this it's telling us that there are 4 beats to the bar. The other four below tells us that the value of one beat is a quarter note. Or, put simply, 4 quarter notes per bar. A bar is the line running vertically through the staff all the way throughout the piece of music. It works in conjunction with the time signature as a sort of visual tidying up. Without these bar lines it would be like driving without white lines in the centre of the road - you'll still reach your destination, but the journey would be an awful and dangerous one. Quite simply, bar lines indicate the end of the four beats and the beginning of the next 4 beats. Of course, music isn't always 4 beats to the bar. For instance, if it was 3/4 we would now have three beats at the value of a quarter note - three quarter notes per bar.

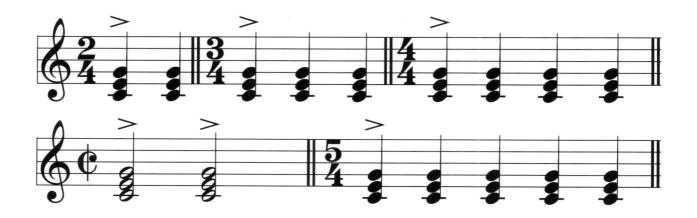

staves and clefs

the treble clef

Staves (singular, 'staff') are made up of five lines and four spaces running parallel across the page. We, as keyboard players, have the major disadvantage of having to read two staves at the same time. The top staff is in the treble clef whilst the bottom staff is in the bass clef. Clefs are used to denote where a certain note can be located at all times - for example the treble clef is also called the G clef. If you look, you'll see that the scroll wraps around the second line from the bottom - the G line. This tells us where the note 'G' should be placed.

the bass clef

The bass clef denotes where the F note is located - thus it can also be called the F clef. You can find the F note line located between the two small dots at the right of the main symbol.

two hands - two clefs

The reason for the two clefs in piano music is really one of tidiness; for if we wanted to play bass notes just using the treble clef then you can see the problems of running out of lines on which to place our notes. We could use ledger lines (little extra lines written above or below the main stave) but just imagine the visual absurdity of this. So two staves are most definitely needed.

Now we know what staves are we must familiarise ourselves with the notes that are placed upon them. Concentrate on the treble clef first, noting little aids like <u>E</u>very <u>G</u>ood <u>B</u>oy <u>D</u>eserves <u>F</u>ood. As you can see by the diagram below these cryptic letters are located on the five lines - this is useful for remembering which note goes where. Likewise, <u>F</u>-<u>A</u>-<u>C</u>-<u>E</u> is what the letters spell in the four spaces; again, very easy to remember.

The bass clef can also be phonetically remembered: <u>G</u>ood <u>B</u>oys <u>D</u>eserve <u>F</u>ood <u>A</u>lways, this is what the five lines could spell out. Likewise, the first three spaces spell the word <u>A</u>-<u>C</u>-<u>E</u> the last space being G. You don't have to use these examples - you can make up your own.

I hope this helps you to overcome the initial fright of having to learn so much detail. You may find this all rather irrelevant at the moment, but I strongly urge you to stick with it - it will pay off in the long run.

F A C E   E G B D F

Every Good Boy Deserves Food

A C E G G B D F A

scales

By now you should know the letter names for all the white notes. So our first scale to learn is C major - which is 8 white notes from C to C. C-D-E-F-G-A-B-C.

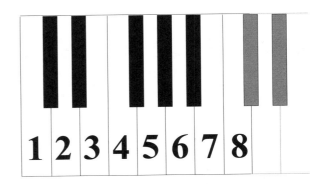

1 2 3 4 5 6 7 8

C major scale - step by step

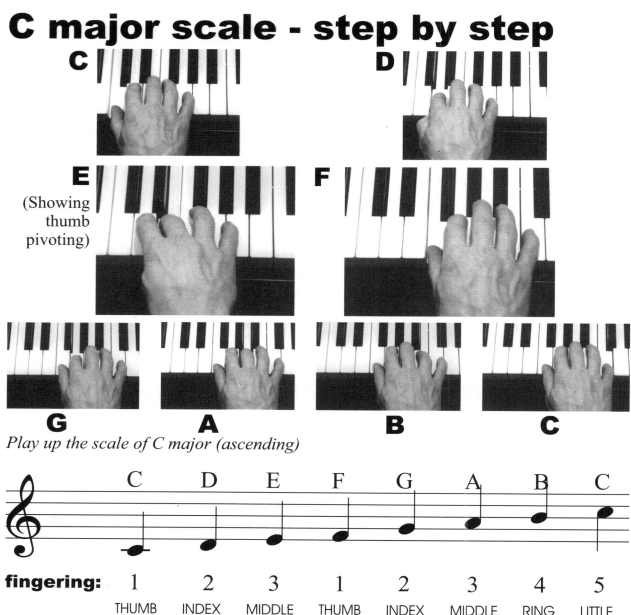

(Showing thumb pivoting)

C D E F G A B C

Play up the scale of C major (ascending)

	C	D	E	F	G	A	B	C
fingering:	1	2	3	1	2	3	4	5
	THUMB	INDEX FINGER	MIDDLE FINGER	THUMB	INDEX FINGER	MIDDLE FINGER	RING FINGER	LITTLE FINGER

To use the correct fingering when playing scales is most important. The right hand fingering for playing this ascending scale is as follows: Play C with the thumb, D with the index finger, E with the middle finger, then whilst the E is being played start moving your thumb under and across to play the F. Your index finger plays G, the middle finger plays A, your ring finger plays B, finally playing the octave C with your little finger. When the scale is descending use the following fingering: 5,4,3,2,1,3,2,1. For the left hand play: 5,4,3,2,1,3,2,1 - ascending and 1,2,3,1,2,3,4,5 - descending.

construction

Let's take this opportunity to see how the major scale is constructed. From C to D is an interval of a whole tone (2 semitones). From D to E is a whole tone. From E to F is only a half tone or semitone. From F to G is a whole tone. From G to A is a whole tone. From A to B is a whole-tone. From B to C is a half tone (semitone). So let's write down this formula which holds true through all the major scales: Keynote, whole, whole, half, whole, whole, whole, half.

So, let's say you want to learn the scale of G major, how do we go about it? Well, look at the formula and apply it. But your starting note (root) will now become G instead of C. So, to explain in detail:

Our root note is G then the formula says we must go up a whole note which is to A, then it says go up another whole note which is B. Now we see the formula says only go up a half note which is C. then it says we have to go up a whole note again which is

D. Now up another whole tone to E. Then it says go up another whole tone - Oh dear, but that means a black note! That's right! But what letter name can we give it? Well, alphabetically our next note should be F, but we're not exactly on the F are we? We've had to raise it a semitone to fit the formula. So we could call it F raised but the correct term is F sharp written down as F♯. Back to our formula and we see we have to go up another semitone which is G. And that's how you can work out any major scale - try it. The fingering for G major is the same as C major. Fingering will vary according to which scale is played.

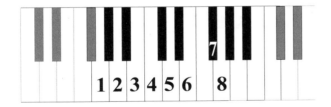

minor scales

The minor scale isn't quite so user-friendly as the major scale, because there are several forms of the minor scale i.e. natural minor,

harmonic minor, melodic minor and dorian minor. I'll just concentrate on the natural minor to make things less confusing.

the natural minor

The natural minor (or relative minor) is so called because it is closely related to its major form. It shares the same notes but in a

different order. This should make it clearer:

C Major:
C D E F G A B C
A Minor:
A B C D E F G A

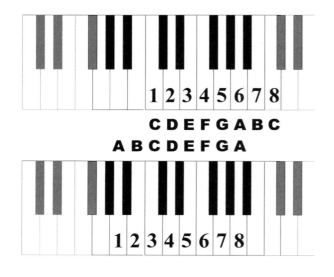

You can see now why this is called the natural minor. The formula for working out other natural minor scales is as follows: from the major key note, in this case 'C', go down 3 semitones or, more correctly labelled, a minor 3rd, this note being 'A'. This gives you your root note for the natural minor. The beauty of the natural minor is that once you've found your root note the rest of the scale uses the same notes as its major i.e. A, B, C, D, E, F, G, A - simple! I'll give the same explanation but this time working out what the natural minor is for G major.

G Major:
G A B C D E F♯ G
E Minor:
E F♯ G A B C D E

the minor pentatonic

This scale is a life saver for any improvising musician. It sounds great if it's not overdone. This is the very fibre of Rock and Blues music. Whereas some of the classical minor structures (harmonic, melodic) won't have any relevance to your modern ears; The pentatonic, on the other hand, will seem instantly satisfying and modern sounding. Here's the formula: The root is D, up 3 semitones (minor 3rd) to F, up a tone to G, up a tone to A, up another minor 3rd to C then another tone to D. Experiment in other keys using this pentatonic minor formula. The reason I choose D pentatonic is because there are only natural notes to play - but you must get used to the black notes. Try C pentatonic minor: C, E♭, F, G, B♭, (C), the sign ♭ means FLAT or lowered one semitone.

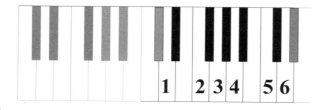

the chromatic scale

This is a scale that uses twelve notes to the octave instead of the usual 7 notes. For example, here is C major C-D-E-F-G-A-B = 7 Notes.

Our chromatic scale starting from C would look like this:

C-C♯-D-D♯-E-F-F♯-G-G♯-A-A♯-B
= 12 notes

This is a very useful scale for playing notes that are not necessarily in the chord being played but will give you many more options when it comes to improvising. You merely take small sections and use them to make a descending phrase from say E to C more interesting by giving this fall a little more tonal colour i.e. E-E♭-D-D♭-C, see fig. 1, use ascending phrases in the same way: C to E, C-C♯-D-D♯-E, see fig. 2.

Take note of the correct fingering and these little fills will be much easier to execute. Practise over two octaves or more once you feel confident enough. Then practise from starting notes other than C. This will prove if you've *really* understood and memorised the correct fingering.

fig. 1 E E♭ D D♭ C
fig. 2 C C♯ D D♯ E

fingering: 2 3 1 3 1 2 3 1 3 1 3 1 2

The easy way to remember this fingering is: Right Hand - 2nd finger on C and F
Left Hand - 2nd finger on B and E
All other notes are 1st finger (thumb) = white notes, 3rd finger = black notes, easy!

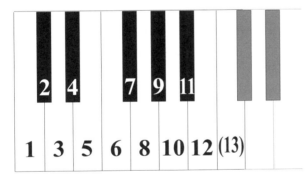

the arpeggio

Briefly this means the notes of a chord played one after another, instead of simultaneously. For example C major played as a chord looks like fig. 3 and played as an arpeggio looks like fig. 4.

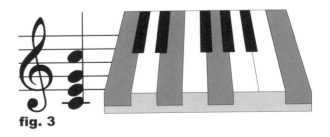
fig. 3

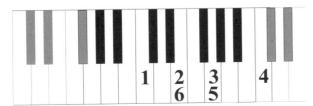

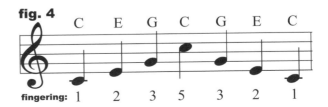
fig. 4 C E G C G E C
fingering: 1 2 3 5 3 2 1

It's worth taking time out to practise arpeggios in as many keys as possible. If you really want to explore this fascinating and important area of keyboard study, then look out for my pamphlet detailing all the keys and all fingerings (from R. & C. Gregory Publishing Limited).

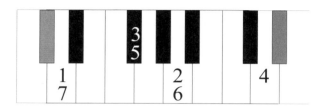

variation on D major arpeggio

key signatures

The key signature is a useful device mainly brought into existence because of tidiness. Just imagine how many individual flats or sharps you would have to read for each individual altered note throughout a whole piece of music. So, instead of writing individual flats or sharps that keep recurring throughout the piece, we simply put a guide at the beginning of the piece to indicate that all the 'B's you play will now become B♭. This information gives us a key centre, hence the term key signature.

Key signatures also make it easy to tell other musicians which notes you are using. They will also know from this which chords you are likely to be playing.

fig. 1:

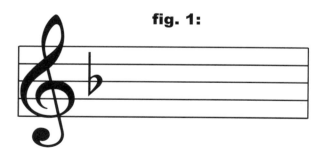

fig. 2:

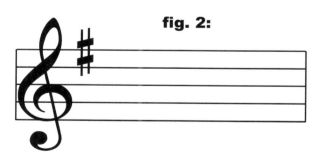

Fig. 1 shows how to indicate a key which has one (permanent) flat note - B♭. This indicates a key of F major (see above).

Fig. 2 shows how to indicate a key which has one (permanent) sharp note - F♯. This indicates a key of G major (see above).

LEARN YOUR KEY SETS; KNOWN AS KEY SIGNATURES								
C MAJOR - All Natural Notes		C-D-E-F-G-A-B						
G MAJOR	1 sharp note	G	A	B	C	D	E	F♯
D MAJOR	2 sharps	D	E	F♯	G	A	B	C♯
A MAJOR	3 sharps	A	B	C♯	D	E	F♯	G♯
E MAJOR	4 sharps	E	F♯	G♯	A	B	C♯	D♯
B MAJOR	5 sharps	B	C♯	D♯	E	F♯	G♯	A♯
F♯ MAJOR	6 sharps	F♯	G♯	A♯	B	C♯	D♯	E♯
F MAJOR	1 flat note	F	G	A	B♭	C	D	E
B♭ MAJOR	2 flats	B♭	C	D	E♭	F	G	A
E♭ MAJOR	3 flats	E♭	F	G	A♭	B♭	C	D
A♭ MAJOR	4 flats	A♭	B♭	C	D♭	E♭	F	G
D♭ MAJOR	5 flats	D♭	E♭	F	G♭	A♭	B♭	C
G♭ MAJOR	6 flats	G♭	A♭	B♭	C♭	D♭	E♭	F

LIVING TOGETHER

PLAYING AND WRITING KEYBOARD PARTS

I want to play a synth riff

OK, how do you go about it?

Firstly, if you're inspired by the sound of a riff you like, try and train your ear to recognise the characteristics that make up that particular sound. i.e. is it brassy or percussive, or has it a string-like quality? This is good to do on all records you hear whether you want to play the song or not - once you travel down this road you'll find through all your musical life you'll be analysing - analysing - analysing - you just can't help it!

So we've got near enough the sound we want; What's the next step? Play the tape or CD over and over until you can sing the riff exactly as heard. Go to your keyboard and literally scout for that elusive 1st note. If you can find

that, you're half way there. If you can't find it, don't fret too much, you just have to work harder at training your ear to recognise what note you sing and where that note can be found on the keyboard. Be assured, that note is there.

So let's assume you're a genius and you've found the note, do we do the same for the rest of the notes? Well, not exactly because we now have a starting note and therefore as our riff is a linear phrase (single line riff) we can detect whether the next note ascends or descends from this first note. This should make the job a lot easier. Whatever the outcome of this hit 'n' miss method, it's good to explore music this way and very rewarding if you get it right. It trains your ears for life.

"teaser" two handed synth riff - brass sound.

writing keyboard parts

There are several ways of doing this. If you are doing it from scratch like an artist with a blank canvas, it can be pretty daunting. There is, however, a good way to get a grounding in making up parts using the random 4 chord method:

Choose any 4 letters of the musical alphabet, let's say C G A F. Now it's simply a matter of playing around with these four chords to get a good-sounding, logical progression. This might entail making some chords minor to achieve our aim.

I've decided, in a couple of minutes to make this my chord structure:

C - G - F - Am

using these inversions:

351 513 513 351

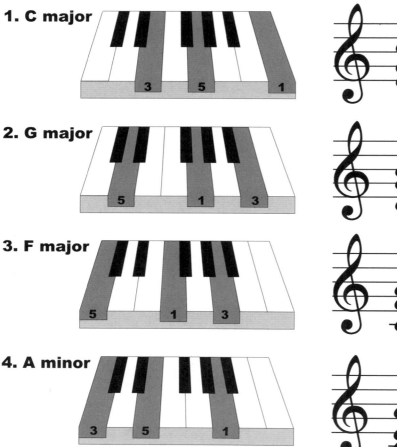

1. C major

2. G major

3. F major

4. A minor

Now try and hum the key note i.e. the note you think would end the part. The note you hum is, hopefully, C. This denotes our key centre or tells us this part is in C major.

As yet we don't know if this is our verse or our chorus. Although these chords don't sound too bad on their own, thinking about what the bass player is likely to play will give you a stronger idea about which direction the part is heading i.e. Rock, Soul, Pop etc. For instance, if the bass were to play the root notes of the chords (see fig 1) then this gives out a sad, soul vibe.

fig. 1

But if we find a note common to as many of the chords as possible, in this case C, play that note over all four chords playing quarter notes - this then gives out a more pop type of vibe.

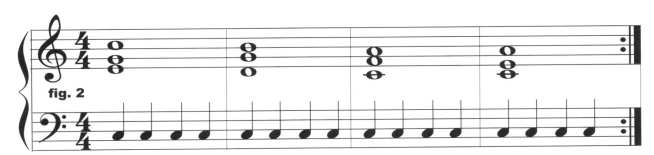

fig. 2

What does sound good in chord and bass structures is what I call the tension note. i.e. a note that gives out a definite tense underbelly sound that lulls you in with its hypnotic pull. See fig. 3; using the 'A' as a root note for the bass and having it playing 8's (eighth notes) gives out a very strong rock vibe.

fig. 3

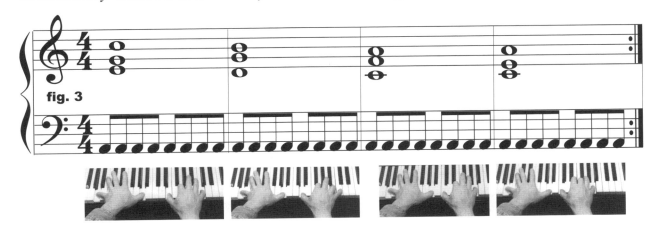

As I like this last example (rock vibe) I'm going to use this as my verse. Still using the same choice of the four randomly picked chords (C - G - Am - F) I'm going to try and come up with a suitably sounding chorus. Because the bass is playing the A all the time this makes our verse more of a minor sounding quality. And a good tip when writing parts is make the chorus major - if the verse is minor or make the chorus minor if the verse is major, this gives the parts more life and

can change up the quality of your chords - always bear this in mind.

This example isn't song writing it's writing a keyboard part. Writing songs requires melody and other structural things which I haven't got time to go into here. Other ways of writing parts may require just a linear riff. (single note line).

Let's say the group have already laid out the chords on guitar and the bass and drums have come up with a matching,

ROCK VIBE VERSE - 105 beats per minute = medium - Play 4 times

fig. 4

fig. 5   **ROCK VIBE CHORUS**   **Play 2 times**

direction. So, as our verse is sounding minor let's make our chorus major. Our verse ends because on A minor, it suggests to me a desire to play a G major - still playing 8's on the bass but with the G note, let's keep up the tension by dropping down a tone with our chord to F but retaining our bass note G (see fig. 5) This then becomes our Chorus. This should give you more of an idea how bass

suitable groove. They are now looking at *you* to come up with that elusive, catchy riff to put the icing on the cake.

Let's continue using the same rock parts but now we have to find a suitable riff. Rather than fiddling around on the keyboard in the vain hope you'll accidentally come up with a masterpiece; try sitting back and close your eyes and really *listen* to what the other band members are doing. Then just sing out your ideas until you land upon a good one. Don't just sing it once, otherwise you'll lose it. Sing it over and over until it's buried deep in your mind. Now go to your keyboard and try and play it. If you can play it, try and write it down on some manuscript paper - don't worry about the rhythm just yet but get the note heads on that paper as quick as you can (see fig. 6).

Then, afterwards, you can work out the rhythm if you think it's important for you to remember it. Sometimes seeing the note heads is enough to bring back to mind the original rhythm. But I would strongly urge you to practise writing down your rhythm. This is how my riff looks when completed with its correct rhythm. (see fig. 7)

fig. 6 (rough)

fig. 7 (finished notation)

jamming and the 12 bar blues

The 12 bar sequence or 12 bar blues is one of the commonest chord progressions in contemporary music.

It is very embarrassing not to know this progression as you will often be called on to jam (play without any preparation or rehearsal) with musicians you meet for the first time, using this progression.

It is useful also because it establishes the importance of the chords built on the 1st, 4th and 5th notes of the scale. The key note (1st note or I) is the most important note, followed by the 5th and 4th notes (in that order). Chords built on these notes will sometimes be described as the I chord, the IV (4) chord, and the V (5) chord.

(Roman numerals are used if this is written down.)

These three chords all support and interact with one another to give the illusion that the I chord is the strongest, or the place in the music where the sound is stable and at peace, or resolved.

Although these three chords are traditionally arranged in the order that we know as the 12 bar blues, they can be arranged in almost any order and structure to create an almost infinite number of compositions. Many songs use only these three chords and are lovingly referred to as the 'three chord trick'. (Status Quo fans will immediately relate to this concept.)

12 bar sequence

C - C - C - C - F - F - C - C - G - F - C - G

By referring to the 12 bar sequence as numbers, you should find it easy to work out which chords to play when jamming in

other keys. (Remember Roman numerals are used to represent each chord.)

I - I - I - I - IV - IV - I - I - V - IV - I - V

Remember to use inversions when playing chords! Here are the

chord shapes best used for C major, F major and G major.

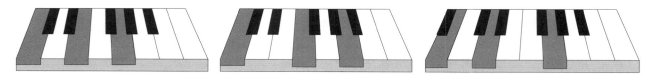

C major   **F major**   **G major**

12 bar bass line exercise

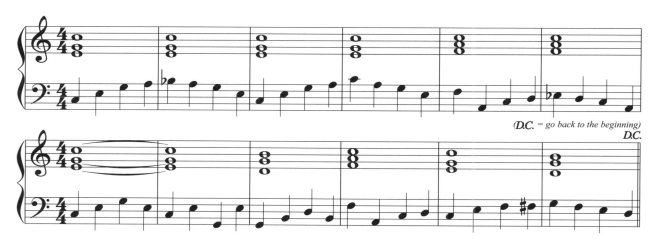

(D.C. = go back to the beginning)

12 bar top line exercise

chord voicings - a voyage of discovery

The term chord voicing must not be looked upon as another way of saying chord inversion. Chord voicing includes other rarer sounding qualities than just pure inversion of the standard 135/351/513. Indeed, the possibilities in the world of chord voicing is endless; I can only walk you briefly through this world, but I hope you can pick up something along the way.

II - V - I PROGRESSION

To simplify things, the examples I've shown here are in the key of C (major or minor) this will allow you to make your own comparative analysis when

Voicing chords using other, rarer, notes from the scale such as the 6th, the 7th and the 9th go to add a certain colour to our chords.

Try these voicings and add a root

experimenting in other keys. The first example I've shown is known (in abbreviation terms) as a II - V - I pattern. Which means, in the key of C major, we play the second chord which is D minor; the fifth chord which is G major; and the one or first chord which is C major.

So let's take this sequence of D minor G major and C major. Normal block chords would be: D minor (DFA) G major (GBD) C major (CEG). (see fig. 1)

And to use standard inversions on these chords we could play them like this:
D minor (DFA) G7 (DFB) C major (EGC). (see fig. 2)

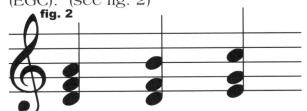

note with your left hand: D minor F, (below middle C), C (middle C), and the E (above middle C). The abbreviation would be 3,7,9, in other words, the 3rd note of the D minor scale; the 7th note of the D

EXPERIMENT WITH NOTE SPACING IN CHORDS (THE CHORD WIDTH)

You can create an almost endless variety of sounds and tonal colour by varying the octave placement and therefore the distance apart of each note. The opposite example shows the chord progression using inversions and wider spacing.

It is easy to experiment with the 'chord width' and this will also help you find your notes on the keyboard.

Spacing chords in different ways can make all the difference in matching the tone colour of the chord/inversion with the sound on your synth or piano.

Even though these examples are written on one staff, divide the notes between two hands for ease of playing.

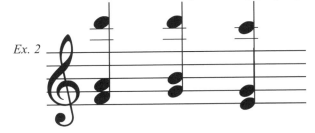

minor scale and the 9th note of the D minor scale. For G7 we could use the voicing 7, 3, 6, this would give us F, (below middle C, B (below middle C) and E (above middle C). In other words the 7th note of the G major scale which, alphabetically is F (we don't raise the note to F♯ because our II - V - I pattern is in the key of C major and therefore must adhere to the C major alphabet.) The 3rd note of the G major scale which is B and the 6th note of the G major scale which is E. For the C maj chord (the key chord) we could use the voicing 3,6 9. This would give us E, (below middle C), A (below middle C) and D (above middle C) See how much we've coloured the sound of these three chords by using the power of voicing.

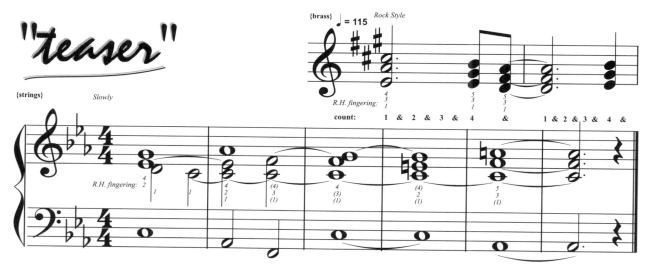

objective voicing

Try to keep your voicings roughly in the area of middle C, this will prevent your chords sounding muddy. The example above would be used to accompany a singer or soloist, but shouldn't be used if playing with a bass player; as the use of root notes on the left hand would certainly be heard as surplus to requirements and, more importantly, would definitely cloud the musical waters you wish to remain clear.

When playing with a bass player who's breathing fire down your neck, it's time to rethink your choice of voicings!

two hand voicing

It's no good to just duplicate with your left hand what you are playing with your right; this is a very poor form of voicing. So try the following examples of playing Dm, G7 and C maj7 and don't worry that it sounds thin; remember, the bass player's note(s) are still to be added and this will certainly fatten up the overall sound.

Dm   G7   Cmaj7   Dm   G7   Cmaj7

a 12 bar can be exotic

Try the following voicings for a 12 bar blues pattern. This is for left hand only, leaving you free to try your hand at solo work. You could also use your right hand for these voicings if you had to supply the bass line yourself.

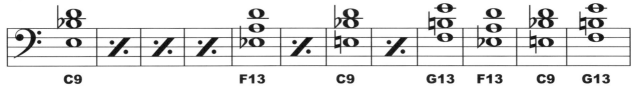

C9   F13   C9   G13   F13   C9   G13

jazz style voicing

It may be asking too much of you to understand fully the complexities of jazz voicings at this stage, but the example below will give a good indication of what voicings are capable of.

Record the bass notes, or find a bass player who will play the roots to these chords and see how well they sound as you play along with them.

B♭ maj7 $^6_9$ E♭ maj9   C7♯5♭9   F9   B♭ maj7 $^6_9$

I want to back myself singing

accompaniment (*jazzers call it comping*)

I wouldn't suggest learning songs using the synth riff method as this requires the use of chords (not single notes). Listening harmonically (two or more notes played together) is much harder to do than listening to a linear phrase (single note line). So we have to know our chords - it's back to those families again (Major and Minor). Once you've de-mystified the world of chords there literally isn't any song you won't be able to work out and, hopefully, play - this style of playing is called accompaniment. For now, let's fantasise that you really understand the construction of chords, how do you use this to learn songs? The answer lies in the use of busking books - or more specifically, the type of busking

books with chord symbols in i.e. where above the music or words there are symbols that look like this: Cm - Cmaj7 - Fm - D - Gm etc. or the books may have guitar symbols above the music which is equally suitable. An example of these symbols looks like this for C - F - G:

As long as you can count an even 1-2-3-4 and play the chord required on beats 1-2-3 or 4 then, really, you're home and dry. This is the best way of getting off home base and into the big world of keyboard playing. Never underestimate the value of chords. Every instrument and every vocalist relies on them, even the milkman whistling his linear repetitive 'tune *!?' is still wandering through the magic and power of chords.

"teaser"

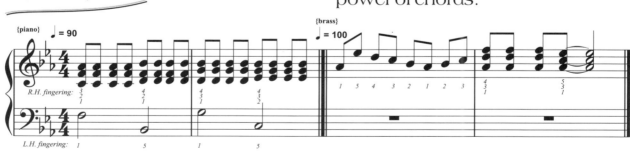

THE SEVEN WEEK ITCH
GETTING INTO A BAND!

what do I play?

This is a good question. Some people know exactly what they want to play - others haven't got a clue. You may want to be able to play a particular piece of classical music, or you may want to just play some synthesiser riffs that you've heard on a dance track etc. Or you may want to utilise the keyboard as a writing/creating tool. Whatever you decide, it's good to have a goal in mind. Most of my students just want to be able to back themselves singing or to be able to back other singers or be part of a gigging band. Whilst these all may seem far away goals on the horizon, it is, nevertheless, easier if you can focus on one spot or one aspect and really study and practise it. This will suddenly bring that horizon a little nearer.

write it down or record it

A useful tip whilst you're experimenting on your keyboard is to try and record all your sessions. It doesn't matter how amateurish or rough it may sound there will very nearly always be a short piece that will sound OK and possibly be useful as a riff or part of an original song. Believe me, many a good riff or chorus has been lost to the world because it was not recorded (or written down) at birth.

Make this a habit - you won't regret it!

being part of a band

The important word here is 'part'. The sooner musicians realise that a band is made up of equal parts and not some mythical hierarchical pyramid (see fig. 1 on the next page) the better!

Good music, like any good band, is greater than the sum of its parts. In other words, drop any urge to be a 'prima donna' or 'star'.

Just fit in. You only achieve good music if you are all locked in to achieve your goal - making great music.

Fig. 1
*not the way
it should be:*

equipment

This never goes wrong at home, does it? Your leads never crackle, your keyboard stand always remains in a fixed state, and your amplifier sounds as clear as an orchestra and as powerful as a rock band. Perfect! Then it arrives at the gig and for some inexplicable reason it becomes the most bolshy bit if kit you can imagine. Every lead sounds like chips frying - the keyboard stand is short of a couple of wing-nuts or wobbles around like a jelly - your amazing bit of amp kit sounds like a squeaky violin being pushed through a sack of cotton wool:

<u>Nightmare!</u>

How to avoid pitfall one:

Double up (at least) on all your leads. Carry a soldering iron with you to the gig (I've had to use one many times). If your stand relies on wing-nuts or bolts to hold it together, carry spares, or, better still carry a spare stand. (Money well spent)

Let me try to make your life a little easier by off-loading some of the pitfalls that many of us musicians have come across at gigs or rehearsals.

Fig. 2
*the way
it should be:*

Amplification for Keyboard players, is the heart of disappointing evenings. It doesn't matter how good your performance or how many times you are congratulated by the audience; nothing will cheer you up because you know the sound that you've loved at home and got so excited about just didn't happen at the gig. A useful tip: If your amp is drastically under-powered for the gig, ask the vocalist (nicely) if you can go through the mixing desk or P.A. amp via your line-out. This will save you having to turn up the volume on your own amp too much, resulting in a clearer, cleaner sound.

Your keyboard instrument should be shown total respect at all times. Never use it as a beer-mat or ash-tray; it has an allergic reaction towards both these mis-uses. Don't venture out with your instrument naked - it's not an offence - but it's immoral not to clothe it in a protective flight case.

fitting in

Not as easy or as obvious as it sounds. If you're in a band that has a vocalist, a guitarist, a bassist, a drummer and maybe a sax player - what the hell do *you* play? Is there any room to show off your new-found talents? - No, our job is to supply layers and textures of sound. Like oxygen, it's all around us, we breathe it, we rely on it but it's not a visually obvious thing. So to, is it usually our function to supply the air or atmosphere in the piece of music. Of course they'll be times when we'll be called on to play a masterful piece of solo work - but in general, the role of atmosphere creation should be at the forefront of your thinking. Basically it goes with the job! If you want to be a showman I suggest you buy a microphone and grow your hair!

a variety of species

vocalists - *Prima Donna, Prima Donna*

The most egotistical, insecure brand of people you will ever meet. Always agree with them (if you want to keep your job!). Never tell them they're singing the wrong note - only suggest an 'alternative' one - you get the result you want without silly tantrums that take weeks to heal - be warned; there isn't enough cotton wool in the world to protect the fragile ego of the vocalist.

guitarists - *Maximus Voluminous*

See 'Vocalist', but add volume of immense proportions. This is a possible musical duelling partner - but he'll always win!

When you hear a guitarist saying "A", he's not asking you for a tuning note - what he's saying is "A???" - in other words, he's as deaf as a post! You, too, can share this affliction if you're foolish enough to set up in the same vicinity as our axe hero.

"Turn down a bit", is the most commonly heard phrase any lead guitarist will hear during his apprenticeship. However, do take note of the dynamic style of your guitarist and try to put a little of this flair into your own solo style.

sax players - *Squeaky Nervosa*

Though thin on the ground, they have definitely left their mark. If you want to witness what nervous eyes look like, go and see a sax player who's not at the top of his form. Like a rabbit caught in headlights is how most sax players have to endure their musical performance. Theirs is a life that's filled with glory and good times, if they have mastered their instrument - for others, however, it's total humiliation as they squawk and squeak their way through an evening of bum notes. Be prepared for him/her to look round at you when one of these bum notes is set free - he's trying to indicate to the audience that it's all *your* fault by playing the wrong chord! - As if we would.

bass players - *Tragediceous, tragediceous*

Oh dear, get out the box of tissues. Stories of great sadness and personal doom are some of the lighter moments that the bass player will eagerly off-load to any available ears. Don't set up your equipment too near this breed unless you want to gather information on your 'Samaritans' thesis about suicide potentials.

On a professional level though, bass players usually know their stuff. Avoid doubling-up on the notes he/she's playing - this is very annoying to bass players as it affects the lines they're playing and can even throw their timing. If the music is sounding muddy it's not the bass player's fault, it's more likely to be the fault of the keyboard player encroaching on the bass player's territory.

drummers - *Crashbangeous Humerosa*

The jokers of the pack. They'll make a dull day bright. Because they don't need to learn notes and changes and all the other musical baggage the rest of us have to carry around, they have lots of spare time to put on their latest funny-man videos and fully commit to memory every god damn joke on it! And memory re-call comes at the gig - so be prepared for an ear-bashing.

However, this gives us a chance to assess his timing; if he's too quick or too slow with his punch-line, chances are he's too quick or too slow on his drums as well. A good guide to his timing ability is if the bass player is smiling for 50% of the gig - then the drummer's pretty much OK!

SHOWING OFF
THE ART OF PERFORMANCE!

doing it for real - gigging

It's 8:30 on a Saturday night - a pub in the big city - the expectancy level is high.

You're doing a gig! You're actually doing it for <u>real</u>!

Did you get there early so as to set up your valuable equipment before 'Biff' the drummer starts dictating where your 2 square feet of room are, and where his 20 square feet are?

Hope you took a friend along who's been to all your rehearsals and so knows exactly how you should be sounding in this new environment? It's impossible trying to sound-check yourself.

With excitement comes adrenalin; this chemical reaction will be responsible for all your songs being faster and louder than usual. Your hands might be sweating from heat or nerves or both - take a small towel along and if you can afford it, an electric fan - you'll never regret it.

Don't look down at your keyboard all night - look out front and soak in the atmosphere. You're an entertainer now, they (the audience) expect you to be polite and acknowledge their presence.

Never ever leave your equipment unguarded - especially when packing it away at the end of a gig, that bit of expensive kit will be pinched in seconds - I've seen it happen many times to musicians I've worked with. They wear an expression of someone who's dog has just died.

The main thing is to enjoy your music - never let it become a burden.

the red light district (recording)

It's late at night. Your palms are sweating. Your throat is as dry as a bone. You can't back out now - you're in too deep! Your eyes scan across the vacuum-like room, and there, behind the human fish tank, you register the vacant, snake-like smile of a sub species...

Suddenly, the once small, innocuous-looking, light bulb seems to grow and glow beyond all recognition. Blood red, it spits its rays on you like tiny arrows of doom... "Let's go for a take!"

Welcome to your first time in a recording studio. It really can be a nerve racking experience.

By anticipating what's in store for you on your first session, might just help to eliminate some of the terror of the red light.

Step one: Before leaving home, check your equipment is in good working order. Take spares of everything you have spares of. Spend at least half an hour running through scales and other five finger exercises.

Step two: Leave home early - traffic jams can be expensive for you if you're paying for the session; or expensive for others if you keep them waiting and they're paying.

Step three: Get a good sound check. Don't be satisfied with any old set up. Try going direct to the mixing desk if you're not satisfied with the way your keyboard is sounding through the amp when recorded. If the engineer is very experienced at recording keyboards of various types, then you should have no problems in this area. If not, then it's time to use your ears and be critical about the sound you're after. Have your volume on full; this gives the engineer more to play with, and can help eliminate extraneous hissing sounds.

Step four: Relax and breathe full breaths. You know your part inside out and sideways. What's there to worry about? If you're lucky there'll be at least one rehearsal before the big moment.

Step five: The accumulation of all your prior learning and experience is now to be immortalised. Do it justice! Forget the bogey men behind the glass. Forget that wicked, disabling red light and withdraw into the music. Really BE that music. Channel that adrenalin to your advantage. - you might be amazed at the results when it's all over.

Step Six: You've passed the test and you can throw away those studio L plates. Now it's time to suck up to the engineer and glean as much information as you can from him about the workings of his studio (whilst you're packing away your gear, of course!). This will add to your all round knowledge. The more you know about studios, the less you'll come to fear them.

ARE YOU SERIOUS?
SOME STUFF TO KEEP YOU GOING

You may find the examples in this section very difficult at first. Don't worry - just make sure you're keeping the beat and counting and learn slowly and methodically at first.

If you learn carefully first time around you'll soon be able to increase the tempo!

Good luck with your keyboard playing! Drop me a line (and a cheque) when you make your first million!

an introduction to 16th notes

Sixteenth notes greatly increase your rhythmic and musical potential. With this increase in creative possibility comes a considerable increase in difficulty.

When beginning to learn about sixteenth notes your first goal should be to understand how to divide the beat into four equal parts. Do this by counting; 1 - e - & - a, 2 - e - & - a, 3 - e - & - a, 4 - e - & a.

Practise the following exercises, which illustrate the most commonly used patterns.

When playing patterns or grooves that contain mixtures of sixteenth notes and other elements (eighth notes, quarter notes etc.) always keep the sixteenth note count (1 - e - & - a etc.) going. This will ensure that you play accurately and most important will maintain the consistency of the groove.

triple time - triplets or 12th notes

Triplets are a new concept to you. A triplet means divide the beat into three equal parts. To make this clear, count;
1 - & - a, 2 - & - a, 3 - & - a, 4 - & - a.